Reclaiming the Table...

A 31-Day Devotional

Monsignor Jamie Gigantiello

© 2023 by Monsignor Jamie Gigantiello

Reclaiming the Table
A 31-Day Devotional

Published by Emmaus Press
Craig Tubiolo, Executive Editor

Cover concept, Interior Design and Project Management by Bookcoach.US

All Rights reserved under International Copyright Law. No part of this book may be reproduced or transmitted in any form or by any means, electronic or mechanical— including photocopying, recording, or by any information storage and retrieval system—without permission in writing from the publisher.

Unless otherwise noted, all Scriptures are taken from New Revised Standard Version Bible: Catholic Edition, copyright © 1989, 1993 the Division of Christian Education of the National Council of the Churches of Christ in the United States of America. Used by permission. All rights reserved.

The New Revised Standard Version, Catholic Edition, has the imprimatur of the United States Conference of Catholic Bishops (September 12, 1991) and the Canadian Conference of Catholic Bishops (October 15, 1991).

ISBN: 979-8-9867029-1-9

Printed in the United States of America

Table of contents

Dedication — 4

Introduction — 5

   Food: Bringing People Together — 10

   Friends: Joy in the Journey — 27

   Family: United in Love — 42

   Faith: Building Strong Foundations — 59

Afterword — 76

   Recipes from Readers — 81

Dedication

I dedicate this book to my mother Angela, who was devoted to Saint Jude and prayed to Him for my vocation to the priesthood. My mother was a true inspiration throughout my life and was the first to teach me how to love and how to cook. Mom also taught me the importance of breaking bread together with people you love, family and friends, who were the ingredients that fostered my vocation. Thank You Mom and see you in heaven!

Introduction

As the family goes, so goes the nation and so goes the whole world in which we live.
—Pope Saint John Paul II

Like a flavorful, nourishing spiritual meal, the following meditations and ideas are meant to be chewed on, pondered, discussed, and prayed about. I have included a relevant passage of Scripture to introduce each meditation, as well as a piece called "Reaching In" which is food for thought that suggests realistic ways to put the day's meditation into practice. It is followed by "Reaching Out," a simple prayer that reaches out to God for guidance to apply each day's meditation to our life. In a time when so many struggle with a "meaning deficit," but refuse to turn to God, who is the source of meaning, nourishing our spirits has become more important than ever. The following devotional is meant to be shared at the family table and used to nourish who we are, bring us closer to the Lord, and inspire us to live deeper in His reality.

There's no question that when you bring food, friends, family, and faith together good things happen. It may not bring fun and laughter to the table, but it definitely brings joy! That's because whenever you come together, you can't help but share your heart as you talk at the family table. As you discuss the food that you're eating, amidst the "Ooooos" and "Ahhhs" over a delicious meal, it brings back a lot of old times and precious memories. We always feel that the good old days were days that were more fun, more carefree, and less stressful—it's what made them good. We were kids then and had no kids as we do now along with the responsibility of caring for them. And when we come together now as adults around the table, no matter how broad our shoulders are, the weight we carry in life now seems to get us reminiscing about those good old days together...

As we do, we sometimes find ourselves reminiscing about the food that we're eating as its scent fills the house and its flavor is so mouthwatering that we can't get it into our mouths fast enough—it just takes us back to who made it... In the course of our conversation, how many times do we hear accolades like, "My grandmother (or my mother) made the best meatballs, oh, they were to die for!" Maybe they were and maybe they weren't, but as their taste lingers in our memory, what those meatballs do is bring us back to the past when we were kids. The next thing you know, we're reminiscing about the fun times we had, so, it does bring joy and laughter to our hearts and warm thoughts to our minds as everyone weighs in with their memories. When we do find ourselves dialoguing along those lines, a lot of times we wind up joking about who's recipe it is—"No, that was Betty Crocker!" "Whoa, no way, it was my recipe!" "You're both wrong, that was Mom's recipe, can't you tell?!"

One of the most beautiful things about sharing a meal, however, is that a time-tested old cliché comes to life through the experience, making it so much more than the food we eat. The old saying goes, "You come to the table as a friend, but leave as family!" And it is so true, because you're spending quality time that reaches deeper than a good meal. We all pull up a chair, enjoy some food, maybe have a glass of wine, and begin to share life stories with their ups and downs... Sharing a meal just seems to make opening up easier and can't help but create bonds and friendships with people. It has an incomparable knack for strengthening relationships, so, the table is very important; because its focus is not so much about the food we eat as what we share with one another.

And that's really how we live out our faith because when someone opens up and shares life's ups and downs but there are more downs than ups, you can reach out and build them up in Christ—nourishing their souls as well as their bodies. Today's high-paced world borders on being toxically busy and the table is the greatest opportunity that's left for us to unplug and share quality time with people. But we have to make that opportunity work for us. How many times do we hear that parents don't sit down to share meals with their children or that the family table has become more of a relic than a relationship-builder, and any number of similar horror stories. Parents today often don't know what's going on in their kids' lives but maybe if they spent more time at the table with them each day, they could speak into their kids' lives in a more meaningful way. And perhaps the intensifying number of children going astray would subside.

While food, friends, family, and faith have a rare unity about them, basically the most important aspect of the four is faith. When you think about it, you can live without family, you can live without friends, and you can even live without food for a season, but faith is indispensable because it impels us to live with one another—sharing life with one another in God's love.

In the Gospels, Jesus came to create a community—a Kingdom of love that is characterized by harmony among people who live together with the grace to care for one another as He cares. Jesus was all about relationships—the deeper the better! Eating with friends, visiting families; He was a man connected to this world's pain and joys. And that was His mission, to bring peace to His followers and lead them in the right direction, giving them a future with hope (Jeremiah 29:11) that flowed into eternal life. Jesus was and is committed to guiding us, showing us how to live and what our responsibilities are. He doesn't leave us in the dark but explains and guides us to what it means to be His follower. I think today, faith tries to do that same thing and we cannot do it alone. We need people; friends, and family to help us with their support and guidance to strengthen us—and they need us as well. Enter the meaning of a meal—it doesn't just sustain our bodies; it deepens our connection, nourishes our souls, and inspires us to follow Him and reach out as He did.

Each entry is meant to be read thoughtfully during family gatherings at the table and savored like a like a gourmet meal—not rushed through but appreciated. We encourage you to make it a family event that each member participates in by reading and facilitating the discussion at whatever their level of comprehension might be. Other family members can ponder what it means to "reach in" and further thoughtful dialogue by sharing their insights openly around the table.

All these "ingredients" combined together are a recipe for meaningful, scriptural, and lasting relationships. It will help families reclaim the significance of the table as it once again takes its place as a centerpiece of the Covenant love shared by families. Under the guidance of God, our hope is that this tradition will triumph and continue far beyond the initial 31 days this devotional shares.

So, let me invite you to turn off all the phones and come, embark on this journey with us as we endeavor to rekindle the essence of gathering at the table. Additionally, we should emphasize that each passage is meant to be read during family gatherings at the table, with electronic devices set aside. Furthermore, we encourage the idea that different family members take turns reading and leading the discussion each day, in the hope that this tradition will persist beyond the initial 31 days or a single month, helping us truly reclaim the significance of the table. Lastly, we encourage our readers to ponder the concept of "Reaching In" and then openly share their thoughts around the table.

Food

Bringing People Together

Food holds a special place in our lives and has the power to bring families together. In this devotional, we will explore the significance of food beyond its physical nourishment. Drawing from rich biblical imagery and compelling narratives, we will discover how meals became occasions for fellowship, celebration, and spiritual connection. From the miraculous provision of manna in the wilderness to Jesus' Last Supper, we will explore the spiritual depth that can be found in sharing meals with our loved ones. Through reflections on gratitude, hospitality, and the art of gathering, we will learn how to create meaningful food experiences that not only satisfy our physical hunger but also feed our souls.

Day One

*Jesus said to them, "I am the bread of life.
Whoever comes to me will never be hungry,
and whoever believes in me will never be thirsty."*

John 6:35

Meditation

There are those who say that faith and food really go hand in hand, and I think they make a fair point. If we look at both the Old Testament and the New Testament, the Scriptures use food as a way of teaching, as a way of bringing people together. The Old Testament talks about how God provided food for those who were searching and those in need. And in the New Testament, Jesus always used the table to bring people together to teach, and ultimately used bread and wine to become His body and blood – His presence among us. No matter how busy Jesus was, He always took time to sit down and to eat, not only with His friends, but also with His enemies. He used a meal to break down walls and bring people together, transforming a meal into a teaching moment. A meal is a way that people come together. And because it brings people together, Jesus used the table as a means of sharing His life and His teachings and His purpose with those who were searching. And this was all accomplished at the table

Reaching In

Consider the ways you can use a meal to bring people together to live out your faith, break down walls, and share the life and teachings of Christ.

Reaching Out

Lord, show me how I can use my creativity to help people come together and share your life and love with a meal. Amen.

Day Two

*One of the scribes came near and heard
them disputing with one another,
and seeing that he answered them well, he asked
him, "Which commandment is the first of all?*

Mark 12:28

Meditation

Gathering at the family table can be even more than a place to share a meal and discuss the highs and lows of our day. It can also be a great place to "chew over" what God means to us individually and as a family in today's world as we commune over a shared meal. If we look at both the Old Testament and the New Testament, the Scriptures use food as a way of teaching, as a way of bringing people together. Just as Jesus brought people together and talked about His mission to point people to God the Father, we can also discuss our purpose in life and how God factors into it. And in the New Testament, Jesus always used the table to bring people together to teach, and ultimately used bread and wine to become His body and blood—His presence among us. The beautiful thing about this is that though the table isn't the right place for a sermon or an evangelistic "message," it is the perfect place to just talk—which is what Jesus so often did. It is the place where members of the family will feel most comfortable simply discussing their beliefs and ideas even if they are not Christians yet, and pondering their faith if they are. The table is an opportunity we can make the most of to help our family understand the gospel message it non-threatening way as we sit down comfortably and casually enjoy a meal with one another.

Reaching In

Discuss the unique ways God has made a difference through the highs and lows of the day and how the day would have been different without faith.

Reaching Out

Lord, open the eyes of my understanding that I might see You moving in my life both through the ups and downs. Amen.

Day Three

Beloved, I do not consider that I have made it my own; but this one thing I do: forgetting what lies behind and straining forward to what lies ahead,
Philippians 3:13

Meditation

Because the time that we spend at the table is generally extremely informal, it gives us an opportunity to really get to know one another—to observe each other's actions, moods, and feelings... To be all there and completely present, so we can observe and read between the lines enabling us to see what someone is really going through. Additionally, we learn through each other's actions and the conversations that we have. A lot of times we can read into where a person is at in their lives through the casual conversation unique to a meal. It is very revealing and frequently what hides between the lines of life pushes its way onto the lines of someone's faith life, their social lives, and if they're going through any difficulties in their lives that can often be picked up at the table as well. Pope John Paul II observed, "As the family goes, so goes the nation and so goes the whole world in which we live." At our meals, God gives us the opportunity to be to be fully present with one another and share with one another. It is a rare gift that should never be taken for granted and always lived out for the Lord.

Reaching In

As you gear up for your meal, can you ponder the meaning of your mission as you share the table with your family? Do you slip into the temptation to approach the meal in a mundane manner as perhaps one more thing on your "plate" that you need to take care of? Or do you regard mealtime as a ministry and calling from God—a gift to deepen and strengthen relationships and speak into one another's lives? How can you explore ways you can move purposefully from the former and strengthen the latter?

Reaching Out

Dear God, there are so many distractions in this world I ask for your empowering to be all there, fully present, and completely given to you and the task at hand as we break bread and share the food you've provided and the door you've opened. Amen

Day Four

> *...for what is prized by human beings is an abomination in the sight of God.*
>
> **Luke 16:15b**

Meditation

We live in a deeply troubled world that is often distracted by that which tends to promote temporal values (see 1 John 2:16). Sadly, so many seem swept up in diversions which are not ultimately satisfying in their quest for meaningful lives. The one place where people really sit down and find time to relax and remember to breathe again is obviously at the table when they share a meal. Obviously, we all biologically need food to live, but when we eat with one another, it not only strengthens our friendships, but it also gives us an opportunity to open up and share our innermost feelings and thoughts and what's going on in our lives.

On the flip side, it gives those we are sharing a meal with the opportunity to do the same. And it gives us that time to be with one another, to be present to one another, something our harried pace seems to strip away from us. So, the food that we need to keep us moving forward in life gives us the time to be with people and to share and fill each other's needs. We fulfill our biological needs, but we also fill our friendship; our dependence on one another. As we open our hearts and minds to one another in true faith and vulnerability, we let the other person know that we are there to listen and to help them with whatever difficulty they may have in their life. Many times, people use the expression, "We come together at the table as friends, and we leave as family." I have found that to be absolutely true, the time out that a meal provides is a grounding dynamic that brings the "true north" of our faith back into focus somewhat and deepens our relationships.

Reaching In

It has been said that "The Kingdom of God is relationships." Consider the ways a meal affords you the opportunities to build, deepen, and enrich relationships. How can you practically apply your ideas to your meals? If Jesus were to stop by for dinner, what would you serve? What do you think He'd like to eat?

Reaching Out

Dear Lord, help me to see relationships the way You do and craft my meals accordingly. Teach me how I can use my meals to establish more meaningful relationships both with one another but more importantly with you. Amen.

Day Five

Jesus answered him, "It is written, 'One does not live by bread alone."
Luke 4:4

Meditation

We obviously need food to sustain our lives, but it's more than a staple of life, it also offers up the opportunity to feed one another. I don't mean by simply providing meals to family, friends, or those in need—which are beautiful expressions of love and care in and of themselves. What I'm getting at is living out the Word of God and not only feeding each other with a hearty meal, but feeding one another with our presence, with our love, with our concern for one another, and our willingness to be with one another. And since eating is not optional, why not use that opportunity to spend it and to be with people that are important to you at the table?

As Christians, enjoying a meal together holds a deep significance that stretches far beyond "Mom's home cooking." The meal, as seen through the eyes of Scripture, is viewed as a time of fellowship, unity, and shared blessings. Inspired by Jesus Christ's example, Christians believe that meals both foster communion between believers as well as God and humanity.

That is because sharing a meal fosters a sense of community, breaking down barriers and promoting love, hospitality, and mutual care. It is an opportunity to express gratitude for the provisions of God and to honor His presence through prayer and thanksgiving. Ultimately, Christians should view eating together as a sacred act that nourishes both the body and the soul, strengthening relationships and deepening our faith.

Reaching In

In what ways do Jesus' words, "Human beings cannot live on bread alone," apply to the idea that a meal is more than "Mom's home cooking?"

Reaching Out

Lord Jesus, show me how I can take the lead in making mealtime more than just food for the body. Amen.

He gives food to every living creature; his love is eternal.
Psalm 136:25

Meditation

I talk a lot about being present and there's a good reason for that—it is so easy to be distracted and even disconnected from those who mean the most to us in today's world. We can be in each other's company, yet the defiant undertow of our phones draws our hands and hearts to them; it's almost a knee-jerk reaction and has become as involuntary as breathing. Our eyes wind up riveted to our favorite social media sites like they have an overdeveloped gravitational field, and we wind up using our freedom to drift apart from one another instead of reaching out.

But if you think about it, when you sit down to a meal, physically, your hands, your mouth, and your eyes literally have to be present in what you're doing. And all those distractions have to fade away like darkness fades from dawn—it's difficult to eat with a cell phone in your hand and its hooks in your heart. It's difficult to eat when you're absorbed by a sitcom or movie. So, the bottom line is that you have to be present with one another—to be all in with what you're doing. But to be truly present, you have to focus beyond moving the fork from the plate to your mouth and move into the meaning of the moment. And that takes a commitment to leverage the opportunity sharing the table with others offers. It falls to you to reach out and facilitate relationships with the other people that are sharing the meal and break the lingering inertia of life's many distractions. It's easy to look at your phone, but when you're eating together, you have a serious edge to put distractions like that aside. And if it's your family you have a biblical responsibility to draw those lines and place a priority on relationships—and why wouldn't you do that with people that you care about?

Reaching In

What are some realistic guidelines that would limit distractions and help encourage interaction and relationship between family members?

Reaching Out

Father, the breakdown of the family is the breakdown of society. Show me how to counter this blight by strengthening our family and deepening our relationships through our family meals. Amen.

Day Seven

> *But the Lord answered her, "Martha, Martha, you are worried and distracted by many things; there is need of only one thing. Mary has chosen the better part, which will not be taken away from her."*
> **Luke 10:41-42**

Meditation

God had blessed us all with many different gifts, talents, and abilities—however, one of the questions it poses is; how do you use them to serve God? One of the talents that God has gifted me with is cooking and I ran with it in my life. But you do not have to graduate from a culinary school to make a simple (or even not-so-simple) meal. I don't think anyone would argue the point that most of us have perfected the ability to make a delicious sandwich, pour a bowl of our favorite cereal, or cook TV dinners in the microwave at the very least.

And that's all it takes to open your heart, hands, and home to another. To be sure, there are those times when a more sophisticated meal can be a lot of fun and used by God! Overall, however, when it comes to relationships, the heart of God can be seen in the story of the way Jesus addressed Martha's protest in Luke 10: 38-41. The Lord was more concerned with fellowship and connection than all the work Martha was doing for her guests. Translation: fancy meals and the work necessary to make them have their place, but something simple, like a grilled cheese sandwich and tomato soup frees you to get close to the Lord and others.

Knowing your way around a commercial kitchen can be an effective way to serve God by serving others just as we are called to—not only at the table, but in life. I may incorporate my culinary cooking skills to serve people and bring them together, but whatever your skillsets may be, they are a means to an end. The important thing is for us all to keep our priorities anchored to our relationship with Jesus and one another and like Mary, to sit at the feet of Jesus. God will show you how to facilitate that with whatever your skills may be, and as He does, put your whole heart into using them to help others gather at the feet of Jesus.

Reaching In

Discuss the various gifts, talents, and skills each family member feels that they have and talk about how they can be used to bring people closer to Christ and each other.

Reaching Out

Dear Jesus, show me how I can use my gifts and talents to help others sit at Your feet like Mary and help me keep my focus on my relationship with You, not just on those things You want me to do. Amen.

But he said to them, "You give them something to eat."
Luke 9:13a

Meditation

One of the greatest virtues of our faith is hospitality and it is something you see in almost every culture. Hospitality: providing a meal, and making people feel at home by feeding them is a virtue that even extremely primitive tribes have been known to embrace. And from a faith perspective, it's a sign of love because making a meal, however simple or sophisticated, requires giving of oneself. But here's the heavenly hook; we may have to give ourselves, but when we do that for someone, we're expressing our love and desire for that person's highest good—and they can tell. And when we do it in the name of the Lord, it brings the reality of His love from heaven to earth through our heart and hands. It's a way of saying, I love you and I care about you, and I want to do something for you.

When you look at the parables that Jesus shared to teach His followers, you see that He repeatedly used food to create His object lessons. And one of the most meaningful things that resonates with me as a form of hospitality, is when Jesus multiplied a child's donated lunch of five loaves of bread and two fish to feed thousands of hungry people. Jesus wanted to glorify God by extending compassionate hospitality through a miraculous meal—so He did! It shows us that no matter how little we may think we have, we always have enough to share and to give to other people. The simple reality is that we're sharing the Word and heart of God through our hospitality so if we have enough to feed five, we have enough to feed six. We want to be faithful stewards of all God has blessed us with and stewardship is about caring for the blessings and gifts that God has given to us. And the way we thank God for those blessings is to walk in His heart of hospitality and share what He's shared with us. It gives us that time to be with one another, to be present to one another, something our harried pace seems to strip away from us.

So, if you want to put legs on this lesson, when you're making a meal, think about the other people in your world, near and far and make a little bit extra like to take to maybe the single mom or lonely woman down the street whose golden years aren't so golden.

Reaching In

Brainstorm creative ways you can use hospitality to express the love of God to those in your sphere of influence. Discuss things like going the extra mile and don't just make a meal but invite someone who cannot reciprocate over for dinner.

Reaching Out

Lord of love, help us to trust you enough to be the answer to our own prayers and pay the price to share your heart with those who are hurting or in need in practical, loving ways. Amen.

Friends

Joy in the Journey

Laughter, joy, and playfulness are vital ingredients for a thriving family. In this devotional, we will explore the importance of fun and the way it strengthens our relationships. Through biblical examples and enduring wisdom, we will discover that God delights in our enjoyment of life. From the simple pleasures of nature to the celebrations of festivals, we will uncover opportunities to infuse our family life with laughter and lightheartedness. As we dive into this devotional, let us rediscover the childlike wonder within us, create lasting memories with our loved ones, and embrace the joy that comes from living life to the fullest, all while honoring God and His design for family values.

You are my friends if you do what I command you.
John 15:14

Meditation

As I ponder the gift of friendship, it occurs to me that friends are both a want and a need! In fact, as God formed the assorted nuances of the earth and the remarkable expanse of the universe including the heavens and land masses, wildlife, vegetation, and all the rest, upon putting the finishing touches on many of them the Bible tells us, "And God saw that it was good." And as He went through His creative process, curating the features of creation, God created man! And upon crowning His creation with Adam, our Lord surprised us in Genesis 2:18 as He observed, "It is not good that the man should be alone." Among the wondrous distinctions of creation, the divine Designer designed man to need friendship—"it is not good that man should be alone."

The Lord Jesus made a number of observations about Friendship, among them John 15:14, which notes, "And you are my friends if you do what I command you." While at first glance it sounds somewhat rigid, Jesus had actually qualified the statement a couple chapters prior by defining His commandment and its relationship to friendship. "And now I give you a new commandment: love one another. As I have loved you, so you must love one another." The heart cry for friendship began in Eden with the creation of Eve so Adam wouldn't have to be alone—because it wasn't good for him to live without companionship. The Lord Jesus took it to the next level and relegated friendship to a command, but His command was to love one another. That is something we can all aspire to!

Reaching In

Why do you think God designed people to have friends? What are your favorite things to do with your friends? Are there times that you feel like being alone?

Reaching Out

Dear God, help me to be a good friend to those you bring into my life. Amen.

And a second is like it: "You shall love your neighbor as yourself."
Matthew 22:39

Meditation

As Christians, the Bible teaches us to value people and use things. Unfortunately, there are many who do the exact opposite, they use people and value things. Jesus spoke to this in Matthew 6:21 when He said, "For your heart will always be where your riches are." It is an open-ended reality that counsels us to place value on true riches and make sure our priorities are where God wants them to be. In Christianity, friendships are treasured as part of the bedrock of personal relationships with much of our lives built upon them—just as God said in Genesis 2:18, "It is not good that man should be alone."

Friendship is not only esteemed in the Bible, but as Christians, it is a key extension of the second most important commandment which is found in Matthew 22:39 where the Lord echoes Leviticus 19:18. And as such, it is clear that God places considerable value on deep, meaningful friendships where others are treated with love and respect in keeping with the "Golden Rule," found in Luke 6:31, "Do to others as you would have them do to you." The surpassing importance of treating others with the same love and consideration that we would want for ourselves shapes the foundation for cultivating meaningful and supportive friendships. That being said, let us dedicate ourselves to both the Golden Rule and the second most important commandment, treating others the way we want to be treated and loving our neighbors as ourselves.

Reaching In

Talk about some practical ways you can love your friends as you love yourself and treat them as you want to be treated.

Reaching Out

Heavenly Father, help me to be proactive and always on the lookout for ways I can treat others the way I want to be treated. Amen.

Day Eleven

*From everyone to whom much has been
given, much will be required;
and from the one to whom much has been
entrusted, even more will be demanded.*

Luke 12:48b

Meditation

While meaningful friendships often include unconditional love and understanding, the foundation they rest on is mutual trust. It is important to point out that even though trust is the basis of all friendships, there is a different dynamic at play when it comes to trust than there is with love. Love can be completely unconditional; however, trust is not—it is earned gradually through conduct that is "trustworthy" such as steadfastness, honesty, and dependability.

Trust, like love, requires work and vigilance to maintain and must be constantly nourished and proven through the ups and downs of friendship. As fragile as a butterfly wing, the trust that holds a friendship together can be damaged; even shattered, in a heartbeat and yet take a long, long time to rebuild. In the end, the blood, sweat, and tears often required to build the trust necessary to support a meaningful friendship, is a treasure worth the pain, the joy, and the quality of life found in a close friend.

Reaching In

Can you think of different ways a close friendship has been painful at times? Were the difficult times worth the good times?

Reaching Out

Dear Lord, make of me a trustworthy person with godly character and an honorable reputation. Amen.

Day Twelve

Timothy, guard what has been entrusted to you.
1 Timothy 6:20a

Meditation

Trust is certainly the bedrock friendship is anchored to, but why? What does trust bring to the table between friends that makes it an absolute essential for a healthy and meaningful friendship? Let's take a brief look at some of the anatomy unique to trust between friends.

Friendship needs an environment of mutual respect to thrive, and trust creates a belief in one another that enables friends to drop the shields and rest in one another's integrity. An offshoot of this mutual respect is a sense of dependability and loyalty. There is an implied fidelity that friends can rely on one another to say what they mean and mean what they say, be there in the clinch, and keep commitments regardless of how costly they may be. Knowing your friend has your back builds a sense of stability and reliability in the relationship. Furthermore, when you have a friend you can trust, the conflicts that are inevitable in even the best of friendships, are handled with an encouraging approach—both parties understand that no one is deliberately malicious and want to reconcile. Where trust flourishes, good intentions are a given and working together to find resolutions instead of shoring up one's ego, pointing fingers, or criticizing each other lends itself to personal growth and a sense of emotional safety rather than the fear of rejection or judgment.

Reaching In

Talk about additional ways you can think of that trust between friends supports their friendship.

Reaching Out

Heavenly Father, show me ways that I need to do better to become a more trustworthy person. Amen.

Day Thirteen

Do not be deceived: "Bad company ruins good morals."
1 Corinthians 15:33

Meditation

There is a rather humorous story told of a family that moved from a northern state to a state located in the deep south. After making their home there for some time, the family pretty much adopted a typical southern accent, and assumed local expressions, colloquialisms, and habits. They simply conformed to their environment and became like those they worked with, went to school with, and hung out with. Enter the wisdom and warning of 1 Corinthians 15:33, "Do not be deceived: 'Bad company ruins good morals.'" The moral of the story is clear—or it should be, choose your friends wisely and carefully! The importance of surrounding oneself with people who are trustworthy, positive influences, and encourage spiritual growth cannot be overstated because you will become like those you hang out with.

As Christians, friendship is valued and encouraged as an essential of our relationships. However, among the dynamics unique to friendship is vulnerability which exposes you to the influence of those you become close with—for better or worse. While the actual word "friendship" may or may not overtly be mentioned in the Scripture, the concept certainly is—so is the term "friend." Additionally, it comes with guidance, schooling Christians in how to approach friendships and treat others with love and respect. It also comes with its share of warnings such as Matthew 7:15, "Beware of false prophets, who come to you in sheep's clothing but inwardly are ravenous wolves." And while the Lord is referring to false prophets, I don't think it is altogether inappropriate to apply it to false friends.

Reaching In

Are there any tell-tale signs you can think of that might alert you that someone professing to be your friend is actually a negative influence?

Reaching Out

Lord Jesus, grant me discernment and insight to get the read on those who appear to be my friends yet actually are not. Amen.

Day Fourteen

*Bear with one another and, if anyone has a
complaint against another, forgive each other;
just as the Lord has forgiven you, so you also must forgive.*
Colossians 3:13

Meditation

Forgiveness and reconciliation are the axis that the Christian world revolves around. Similarly, they are also the axis that friendship revolves around. 2 Corinthians 5:20 explains that "So we are ambassadors for Christ, since God is making his appeal through us; we entreat you on behalf of Christ, be reconciled to God." And if we are ambassadors for Christ, we certainly want to reach out in that capacity and calling to our friends. In friendships, it is natural for disputes and tension to arise periodically, conflict happens! But as Christians, we are called to forgive and reconcile with each other just as Jesus forgives us and has reconciled us to God. Colossians 3:13 counsels us to, "Bear with one another and, if anyone has a complaint against another, forgive each other;

just as the Lord has forgiven you, so you also must forgive." This is the lynchpin of friendship. An attitude of forgiveness based on the value of the relationship between friends frees us to serve and support one another just as Christ served His disciples. It further enables us to fulfill Galatians 5:13 as Christians, "...but through love become slaves to one another." underscoring the importance of selflessness and a servant's heart in friendships. The bottom line is that friendship for a Christian is a self-sacrificing commitment to the highest good of your friend, treating them with love, respect, and kindness, in pursuit of genuine and loyal companionship. It focuses on living out Ephesians 4:32, "and be kind to one another, tenderhearted, forgiving one another, as God in Christ has forgiven you." Christian friendship is a willingness to support and serve one another through both the good and the bad.

Reaching In

Do you find forgiveness difficult? Why or why not? Discuss something you forgave someone for and then discuss something you were forgiven for.

Reaching Out

Father God, I pray for a forgiving attitude so that I don't miss a beat should someone hurt me—make me like You Lord. Amen.

Day Fifteen

> When David had finished speaking to Saul, the soul of Jonathan
> was bound to the soul of David, and Jonathan
> loved him as his own soul.
>
> 1 Samuel 18:1

Meditation

David and Jonathan's relationship is a beautiful example of what a true, godly friendship should be. It is deeply moving to read how Jonathan, "...came to love him as much as he loved himself," especially in the wake of the way Saul had it in for David. Jonathan loved his neighbor as himself and lived out the wisdom of Proverbs 18:24, "Some friends play at friendship but a true friend sticks closer than one's nearest kin." It is a verse that expresses the importance and example of being committed to a friend with the selflessness, love, and concern anyone would want for themself. It is made of the building blocks foundational for supporting a deep and significant friendship, and a stellar example of the sort of camaraderie and companionship to strive for as a friend. But Jesus didn't stop there, He took it to another level and emphasized the command to love one another, not just as friends but as family in our shared faith. In John 13:34-35 Jesus said emphatically, "I give you a new commandment, that you love one another. Just as I have loved you, you also should love one another. By this everyone will know that you are my disciples, if you have love for one another." It is a statement that reaches to friendships, stressing a love that eclipses self-interest and seeks the well-being of others before oneself communicating the ideal of true friendship and selfless love.

Reaching In

Talk about different ways you can strive to live out this type of friendship. Is there anyone you are close to that you can "ramp up" your relationship with as a friend and take it to another level?

Reaching Out

Dear God, help me be a friend in every biblical sense of the word and love like you love; selflessly, deeply, and meaningfully. Amen.

Family

United in Love

Family is the cornerstone of society, a sacred trust designed by God to provide love, support, and encouragement. In this devotional, we will explore the biblical principles that stress the importance of family values. Through uplifting stories, heartfelt reflections, and practical insights, we will discover how to strengthen our familial bonds and create a nurturing environment for our loved ones. The Scriptures will guide us in building healthy communication, resolving conflicts with grace, and cherishing the unique gifts each family member brings. As we journey through this devotional, may we be inspired to prioritize our families, foster a spirit of unity, and experience the joy that comes from living out God's design for family life.

Day Seventeen

The righteous walk in integrity—happy
are the children who follow them!
Proverbs 20:7

Meditation

It is no secret that the family table has been filled with vacancies in our generation. You hear it over and over again, no matter where you go—gathering at the table is missing, the chairs are collecting dust, and the cutlery doesn't leave the drawer. It is one of the things we can always say that seems to be echoed by everyone. Sitting down as family—wife, kids, and the pet dog mooching under the table, could well be on the endangered list. However, spending time together, especially when a couple gets married, is extremely important and when the kids come along, it's absolutely imperative that their parents are present and spend time with their children. Quality time with kids is one of the bedrock ways to bond and deepen a love relationship with them—there are just no shortcuts. And one of the best ways for kids to spend time together with mom and dad is at the table with their family. It is there, in the causal environment family mealtime offers, that parents can connect with their kids, discover what is meaningful to them, and share the different ways God is real in their own life. Without a doubt, the family table is the perfect place to move from "drive-through" to "talk through."

Reaching In

Discuss the unique ways God has made a difference through the highs and lows of the day and how the day would have been different without faith.

Reaching Out

Lord, open the eyes of my understanding that I might see You moving in my life both through the ups and downs. Amen.

Day Seventeen

But Jesus said, "Let the little children come to me, and do not stop them; for it is to such as these that the kingdom of heaven belongs."
Matthew 19:14

Meditation

The table is so much more than a place to eat, it is one of several safe, enjoyable settings to make memories and share moments with mom and dad where everyone can get to know one another... In order for parents to appreciate discovering what's going on in their children's lives, they have to be present in their them, letting them know that their parents are always there for them. Kids are more perceptive than we often give them credit for, and they get that their parents' lives are harried and busy. They understand that their time is valuable and at a premium. So, the fact that mom and dad make the effort and take the time to sit down and have dinner with their children, play with them, and yes, invest in teaching them right from wrong, sends a powerful message about how much the kids mean to their parents. To put it into this generation's vernacular it gives some serious "street-cred" to the parents love about how much their kids are loved. You could put it this way; nothing says "I love you" like truly sharing your life with your children—which translates to giving your time to them.

Reaching In

Discuss each person's interests, likes and dislikes, at family mealtime and toss around why they are or aren't interested in these various things.

Reaching Out

Dear God, help me to see the treasure You have given me in my children and take a legitimate, heartfelt interest in their lives. Amen.

Day Eighteen

*If you then, who are evil, know how to
give good gifts to your children,
how much more will your Father in heaven
give good things to those who ask him!*
Matthew 7:11

Meditation

The compassion that Jesus showed to families made the value He placed on them crystal clear. And while biological families mean a great deal to the Lord who created them, it is important to point out that families don't just include those who you have a genetic connection with. In fact, Proverbs 18:24b tells us that "...a true friend sticks closer than one's nearest kin." The point I'm making is that as we go through life, we may meet people who we eventually grow to love so deeply that they become our family. Obviously, Jesus loved His mother and the rest of His biological family, but we'd be remiss to think He didn't regard His disciples as family as He poured His life out in service to them. Furthermore, the value the Lord placed on family relationships can be seen through some of His most profound miracles which directly involved family. Jairus pleaded for the life of his daughter, and a widow asked for her son's life to be restored. Of course, there is the amazing story of Mary and Martha's brother, Lazarus, being raised from the dead as well. The Triune God who is Himself a relationship, places surpassing value on the relationships that unite family members.

Reaching In

It is said that the Kingdom of God is found in relationships, and that we are all family in Christ. Talk about why you do or do not agree.

Reaching Out

Lord, show me how to value family relationships the way you do, and different ways I can show those I consider family that I love them. Amen.

Day Nineteen

And now faith, hope, and love abide, these three; and the greatest of these is love.

1 Corinthians 13:13

Meditation

If you are a Christian family, there are a few qualities that will characterize the way you live your life; ways that demonstrate your faith and commitment to God. Let me give you a "heads-up," however, one of them *won't be* perfection—*there are no perfect families*, perfect kids, or perfect parents, that's why we need a Savior! One of them, perhaps the most prominent trait, *will be* love.

Love, compassion, and forgiveness are three intimately connected traits that characterize Christian families, just as they characterize the Christ, they believe in. Through the good times and the bad times family members do their best to love one another just as the Lord loves them. They care about one another's hopes, dreams, and goals, and when conflicts develop, the first order of business is forgiveness and reconciliation—driven by mutual love and compassion.

This often demands parental leadership no matter who is at fault—parent or child. To echo an old adage, "Actions speak louder than words," consequently, it falls to parents to lead by loving example and model both the Bible's teachings and Christ-like, loving behavior. This will play the greatest role in teaching children faith in the God of the Bible, and in providing a nurturing and supportive environment for them to grow in. And it all rests on walking in the love of God!

Reaching In

Toss out the word "love" and talk about its different meanings, such as when a husband and wife fall in love with each other versus the love that good friends have with each other.

Reaching Out

O God, the world will know we are Christians by our love so please help our family to love each other and the people we come in contact with like You do wherever we go. Amen.

Day Twenty

Finally, beloved, whatever is true, whatever is honorable, whatever is just, whatever is pure, whatever is pleasing, whatever is commendable, if there is any excellence and if there is anything worthy of praise, think about these things.
Philippians 4:8

Meditation

Though love for God and each other is the foundation of family, it expresses itself through a number of ways that are basically built upon it. Among these are the moral values and ethical standards taught in the Bible, which include a number of godly character traits. These heavenly attributes include honesty, integrity, humility, patience, selflessness, and purity—to name a few. While it is absolutely incumbent upon mom and dad to teach their children to live out these beautiful moral qualities, their words will fall flat unless they model them from the heart for the kids, in their everyday lives. Their ethical principles are patterned after the teachings and example of Christ and as such, they emphasize godly character traits such as integrity, humility, patience, selflessness, and purity of heart. Furthermore, as parents they will invest time, effort, and energy in setting an example that teaches their children to love God and live according to these same precepts found in person of Christ.

Reaching In

Have each member of the family pick one of the virtues above and describe what it means to them and why. Once they do, have that family member share what challenges they might encounter living it out, and how they will overcome it.

Reaching Out

Dear Lord, give me the grace and desire to stand for you and all that is right so I don't fall for the schemes of those who turn from following godly virtues. Amen.

Day Twenty-ONE

*He will turn the hearts of parents to their children
and the hearts of children to their parents,
so that I will not come and strike the land with a curse.*
Malachi 4:6

Meditation

God is loving and good, so much so, that the heart of heaven beats to make people on earth His friends and friends with one another—and that is all people including children and parents. 2 Corinthians 5:19 puts it this way, "in Christ God was reconciling the world to himself." You can see this incredible power unleashed in the family and why God makes it a priority in Malachi 4:6. Describing parents and children bonding through God's sovereign effort, the verse also illustrates the consequences of parents and their children remaining estranged from each other. In the expanse of His love, the Lord intervenes to bring parents and children together again, stopping the net effect of disaffected families upon a nation—its destruction. Families are *that* important!

Obviously, there are many things that can inspire the bonding of families, and many things that can be done to draw drifting hearts closer together. But, just as raindrops make rivers, every step we take in God's direction brings us closer to His goal of loving and meaningful relationships with Him and each other.

Enter the family table, a far-reaching commitment that can be made to strengthen relationships, work with God to reconcile relationships through Christ, and deepen the love between family members.

Reaching In

Do you feel that joining in family dinner is more than a meal? Why or why not? Acts 20:35 tells us to remember that Jesus said, "It is more blessed to give than to receive." Go around the table and describe how someone blessed you by giving recently. Talk about what they gave and how you think they were blessed by giving? How can you be a blessing to members of your family?

Reaching Out

Dear Jesus, show me ways I can bless others by giving, help me to give from the heart and for the right reasons—like You do. Amen.

Day Twenty-two

*He said to him, "You shall love the Lord your God
with all your heart, and with all your
soul, and with all your mind."*
Matthew 22:37

Meditation

There are certain traits that will distinguish a Christian family from families that do not hold to the teachings of Christ. These are characteristics that reflect their faith and commitment to living according to Christian principles, the Bible, and their love for God. For example, the life of a Christian family will revolve around their faith in Jesus Christ and the various activities that includes. In their quest to follow the teachings of the Bible, it is common to see Christian families attend church, have family devotionals, or attend various seminars and Christian concerts. Additionally, a Christian family will make sure love, forgiveness, and morality are a priority in and out of their home. It is important to live their convictions and follow the example of Jesus with values that may run counter to the culture. Their ethical principles are patterned after the Bible and as such, they emphasize godly character traits such as integrity, humility, patience, selflessness, and purity of heart. Furthermore, as parents they will invest time, effort, and energy in setting an example that teaches their children to love God and live according to the precepts taught in the Bible.

Reaching In

What are some things your family does that distinguishes them as a Christian family? What are some new things you could do to live as Jesus did and honor the Lord?

Reaching Out

Heavenly Father, continually show us new and creative ways we can follow you as a family and share your love with the world. Amen.

Day Twenty-three

Remember your leaders, those who spoke the word of God to you; consider the outcome of their way of life, and imitate their faith.
Hebrews 13:7

Meditation

Among the many things a godly family can do is place a priority on the family meal—but it's not just about the food. Life can grow very busy very quickly and mealtime is a great opportunity for family members to put the brakes on, relax, enjoy good food, and catch up with each other. It gives parents a chance to learn about their children's day at school, discuss their interests and problems, as well as discover anything that's new in their kids' lives. Conversely, mom and dad have the chance to open the door into their world and enlighten their children about the nuances of their lives. In addition to bonding over mom's home cooking, mealtimes also afford the kids an opportunity to pitch in and help clear the table, wash the dishes (or load them into the dishwasher), and lighten mom's load a little. While all the interaction is precious, perhaps the most beautiful thing about the family table is that it communicates the value members have to each other. It may be family mealtime, but it is so much more than the meal. In an age where social media, cell phones, and the clamor of 120 channels on TV dominate and influence both parents and children far more than they should, gathering for a family meal is a breath of fresh air that focuses on true north and what truly matters—going soul-to-soul with each other!

Reaching In

Make a point of having each family member share something that was meaningful to them that day, and explain why, including mom and dad.

Reaching Out

Lord Jesus, please help us to never take one another for granted, but appreciate how special each of us are. Amen.

Faith

building Strong Foundations

In this devotional book, we embark on a journey to explore the significance of faith in the context of family values. Faith forms the bedrock upon which families can thrive and grow. It is through faith that we find strength, hope, and guidance in the midst of life's challenges. Drawing inspiration from the Scriptures, we will delve into the stories of faithful individuals and families, who relied on God's promises. From Abraham's unwavering trust to the faith-filled actions of the early disciples, we will discover timeless lessons that can shape our own family lives. Together, let us deepen our faith, cultivate formidable spiritual habits, and nurture a strong foundation that will sustain our families through every season of life.

Day Twenty-four

O taste and see that the Lord is good;
Psalm 34:8a

Meditation

Our faith rests in the eternal and unchangeable reality that God is good. In a certain sense we take His word for it because it is in His Word, but that same Word invites us to do more than believe what we read in Scripture—it invites us to experience it, to "taste and see" how good He truly is. In essence, He is inviting us to savor His goodness.

And by implication, as we "experience" the goodness of God, that same goodness nourishes us, becoming part of our life and the way we live—giving us spiritual energy and strength. Thus, as we experience the goodness of God, we live the goodness of God bringing it to others by default. Speaking of the leaven of the Pharisees in Mark 7:20-23, Jesus warned that the things which come from our hearts defile us. Conversely, as we taste the goodness of God and it nourishes our hearts, becoming part of us, what comes from our hearts and touches those around us, is His goodness. Let us offer God's goodness to the world around us that others might "taste and see" for themselves through us, how good the Lord is.

Reaching In

Does the Lord's goodness become a living part of us simply by experiencing it or is there more required for us to find out for ourselves how good the Lord is?

Reaching Out

Lord, help me to not just know about Your goodness, but to know it experientially; to encounter it in a way that it might become a part of me and express itself through my life. Amen.

Day Twenty-five

*And without faith it is impossible to please
God, for whoever would approach him
must believe that he exists and that he rewards those who seek him.*
Hebrews 11:6

Meditation

Hebrews, Chapter 11, is known as the "Great Hall of Faith" because it profiles some of the more iconic acts of faith by several of the Lord's most acclaimed servants. Verse 6, in particular, shows us both what these heroes of the faith believed and what we, as Christians, must believe sincerely to come to God. Refreshingly untheological, and about as practical as it gets, Verse 6 tells us that if we want to please God we must do so in faith that He exists and will reward us as we seek Him in that faith.

Let us earnestly reach out to God heart-to-heart, in faith that He exists and will reward our honest efforts to serve Him. Jeremiah 29:13 tells us, "When you search for me, you will find me; if you seek me with all your heart." It is our faith in God that moves us to seek Him with all our heart and thus, we are assured that we will find Him because He will surely reward our reaching out to Him. Because of this simple, yet profound guidance, we can rest in the loving truth that we will find God and His guidance for us as we come to Him in faith. Furthermore, we can live each day in the confidence that our heart cry, hopes, dreams, or problems will not be overlooked or disregarded—that our faith in Him, both pleases God, and inspires Him to act.

Reaching In

Talk about what you think the difference is between just believing that God exists and believing that He rewards those who seek Him.

Reaching Out

Dear Lord, show me how to have a quality of faith that not only believes you exist and will reward me if I seek you, but moves me to make a difference in my sphere of influence. Amen.

Day Twenty-six

But someone will say, "You have faith and I have works."
Show me your faith apart from your works, and
I by my works will show you my faith.

James 2:18

Meditation

James 2:14-26 is an intense discussion about the relationship between faith and actions. It is a conversation that has been front-and-center from the earliest days of Christianity and remains an important spiritual principle to unpack. The New Testament repeatedly makes it clear that we are saved by faith in Christ, relate to God on a daily basis by faith, and our prayers are answered by faith. It begs the question; how do godly or righteous actions factor into this spiritual equation? Do we just sit back on our faith and wait for Christ to return? I don't think so!

Thankfully, James doesn't leave us in the dark but lights the path with a realistic response to the question. "Show me your faith apart from your works, and I by my works will show you my faith" (James 2:18). Have you ever heard the saying, "Actions speak louder than words?" That is because what we do reflects who we really are and what we truly believe. Another deeply relevant old saying is, "Talk is cheap." Anyone can talk the talk, but the heaven-born, down-to-earth truth is that we will *be* what we *believe*. If our faith is real, it will really result in action—we will be what we believe and live out works of faith. Let us show the world what we believe by boldly living out our faith and like James be able to declare with pure, faith-filled hearts, "I will show you my faith by my actions."

Reaching In

Consider the things you have done in the past week. What do they reveal about the difference between what you truly believe and what you say you believe with respect to your faith in Christ.

Reaching Out

Father in heaven, help me to live what I believe and show the world the love of God in Christ through my actions. In His mighty name. Amen.

Day Twenty-seven

For by grace you have been saved through faith, and this is not your own doing; it is the gift of God—not the result of works, so that no one may boast.

Ephesians 2:8-9

Meditation

This is a beautiful passage that makes the spiritual "recipe" for salvation especially clear. The ingredients are God's grace and our faith lived in daily actions. Mix well—and leave the rest to God! In Hebrews, Chapter 11, which we referred to earlier, the Bible, Verses 33 and 34 explain that men of God did remarkable things. "Who through faith conquered kingdoms, administered justice, obtained promises, shut the mouths of lions, quenched raging fire, escaped the edge of the sword, won strength out of weakness, became mighty in war, put foreign armies to flight."

If such amazing achievements were the result of faith in God's promises, how much more are the challenges of everyday life within the reach and grasp of our faith. We may not be going into battle against a hostile nation, but we are embroiled in a battle for the hearts and minds of our children. We may not be up against hungry lions in a den full of them, but Peter warns us that our families are facing down a very real enemy, who, "Like a roaring lion your adversary the devil prowls around, looking for someone to devour" (1 Peter 5:8). It is a battle we can win the same way as our forefathers in the faith—by God's grace through our faith! It is God's recipe for victory whether we are facing down a giant warrior like David, or a giant stack of bills! Faith in God's promises will always win the day!

Reaching In

What battles are you engaged in or what curve balls has life thrown at you lately? Talk about specific promises from the Scriptures that you can stand on in faith and would help you overcome them.

Reaching Out

Dear God, I pray that you would help me walk in your grace and live by faith whether I am faced with a new challenge or filled with joy over an unexpected blessing. Thank you for the grace to believe in your promises. Amen.

Day Twenty-eight

"If the world hates you, be aware that it hated me before it hated you."
John 15:18

Meditation

In today's society, *faith is not easy* to live out or talk about in public due to the fear of being ridiculed. *What is easy* is being intimidated or pressured by the people in our circle who are emblematic of the times we live in and its morality and unbelief. That is because they openly dismiss our faith in God, and frequently we wind up being treated like the punchline of a bad joke.

And as our current generation rises to take their place in the world, our nation, which once embraced God and the Christian faith, has grown hostile and disparaging to our religious beliefs. Among the most widely accepted "spin-jobs" making the circuit across America, is that you're free to practice your religious beliefs but in a quarantined manner, (as if the love of God was a contagious disease). The message is that the freedom to worship God should be confined to either the four walls of your church or kept behind the closed doors of the Christian's home with the immediate family and friends if you want to have a Bible study. 1 John 5:19 speaks to this with both comforting assurance and disturbing truth, "We know that we are God's children, and that the whole world lies under the power of the evil one." John lays the groundwork for that statement in 1 John 4:4 with, among other verses, an encouraging word that assures us, "...for the one who is in you is greater than the one who is in the world," so we truly have what it takes to break out of the box the world is trying to stuff God and His followers into. Well, they got one thing right, the love of God is contagious, and people are aching for it. And while church is a place where you can share your faith, your feelings, your desires, and your beliefs with people who treasure the same convictions, the words of Jesus from Mark 16:15 continue to resonate in our hearts and inspire us, "Go into all the world and proclaim the good news to the whole creation."

Reaching In

What battles are you engaged in or what curve balls has life thrown at you lately? Talk about specific promises from the Scriptures that you can stand on in faith and would help you overcome them.

Reaching Out

Dear God, I pray that you would help me walk in your grace and live by faith whether I am faced with a new challenge, heartbreak, or filled with joy over an unexpected blessing. Thank you for the grace to believe in your promises. Amen.

Day Twenty-nine

*Keep these words that I am commanding
you today in your heart.
Recite them to your children and talk
about them when you are at home
and when you are away, when you lie
down and when you rise.*

Deuteronomy 6:6-7

Meditation

In the Christian family, walking in faith plays a fundamental role in shaping the beliefs, values, and behaviors of its members. It involves living out the principles of Christianity in daily life, fostering a strong relationship with God, and passing on the faith to the next generation. Here are some key aspects of the role of walking in faith in the Christian family. Overall, walking in faith in the Christian family is about actively integrating Christian beliefs into every aspect of family life. It involves living out the Gospel through love, service, and obedience to God's Word, resulting in a strong and spiritually enriched family unit.

Unity and Support: Faith plays a unifying role in the family, promoting love, unity, and support among its members. Christian families are encouraged to pray together, encourage each other in their faith journey, and offer emotional and spiritual support during challenging times.

Service and Outreach: Walking in faith extends beyond the family unit and encourages involvement in serving others and reaching out to the community. Christian families often engage in charitable activities, missions, and volunteering to demonstrate God's love and share the Gospel with others. Understanding God's Design for the Family: Christian families seek to understand and follow God's design for the family as outlined in the Bible. This includes honoring marriage, raising children in the ways of the Lord, and fulfilling specific roles and responsibilities within the family unit. Passing Down the Faith: Walking in faith involves passing down the Christian faith from one generation to the next. Parents strive to be positive role models, share their own faith stories, and create an environment where faith can flourish for their children.

Reaching In

What battles are you engaged in or what curve balls has life thrown at you lately? Talk about specific promises from the Scriptures that you can stand on in faith and would help you overcome them.

Reaching Out

Dear God, I pray that you would help me walk in your grace and live by faith whether I am faced with a new challenge or filled with joy over an unexpected blessing. Thank you for the grace to believe in your promises. Amen.

Now it is evident that no one is justified before God by the law; for "The one who is righteous will live by faith."
Galatians 3:11

Meditation

Among the most important gifts given to a Christian parent, is the call to pass the baton of faith to their child. As believers, we strive to raise our children to live by faith as the Word of God encourages us to. The tragic challenge that our children face in their relationship with the Lord is that it comes down not so much to what they've been taught but to what is caught. Unquestionably, correct doctrine, and solid theology are absolutely essential for the Christian. But theology didn't suffer and die for us, Jesus Christ did. And Old or New Testament Surveys are edifying but they are not the way to know God. Our Lord was very clear in John 17:3, that eternal life comes through knowing God in faith. "And this is eternal life, that they may know you, the only true God, and Jesus Christ whom you have sent."

Reading John 17:3 with the renowned John 3:16, offers a well-rounded understanding of the path to eternal life and meaningful relationship with the one true living God. It is in a parent's knowing the Lord in a way that they live their faith as opposed to just teaching it, describing it, quoting it—in a word, it is the world of difference between knowing about God versus actually knowing Him. When a parent knows the Christ, even if they come up short on the theological side, rendering them unable to teach their children a Bible study, the kids will catch the true faith that their parents have. This is because their parents' faith isn't built upon what they know about God, but rather knowing God, Himself.

Reaching In

Discuss realistic ways to pass the baton of faith in God and faithfulness to God. Also, describe the difference between the two as well as what it means to know about God and what it means to actually know Him intimately.

Reaching Out

Heavenly Father, guide me in the path of knowing You and being faithful to you, and protect me from getting absorbed by the many temptations to know about you. In Jesus name Amen

Day Thirty-one

*No one can come to me unless drawn by the Father who sent me;
and I will raise that person up on the last day.*

John 6:44

Meditation

In John 6:44, Jesus explained that "No one can come to me unless drawn by the Father who sent me..." True faith in God is supported by a compelling spiritual gravitational field that draws those who don't know the Lord. And though they can't help but acknowledge the reality of being drawn, they don't know and can't explain who or what is drawing them or why. But as we reach out to share our life with people that might be of a different background, culture, hostile toward God, or just don't care, it allows God to use that spiritual gravity to draw them through us.

Using the assets that we have been given by God, is a wise and powerful dynamic! As we hear in Scripture on Pentecost, after the Holy Spirit entered the disciples, they were all speaking in different tongues and languages. But then the Spirit enabled them to understand one another in their own tongue. In the same way we can understand and get to know people by reaching out in ways they can relate to, in order to get connected to the unique hunger in their hearts.

Like a mouthwatering meal, it is the way we prepare and season it that makes it different and gives off a fragrance that draws hungry dinner guests to the table. Well, maybe we can take that same thought and say we all have one thing in common—we are all children of God with hungry hearts, created in His image. How we act as children and how we live as children may be different, but basically, we're united in the same struggles and longings in this life. So, using the gravitational field we have been gifted with from heaven to deepen relationships with both those who love the Lord and those who love darkness, creates a spiritual fragrance that is sure to draw hungry hearts to His table.

Reaching In

Do you feel that there is a unique spiritual voice or momentum within you that calls and reaches out to others? What can you do differently and how can you live in a way that voices this heart cry of heaven and draws others, whatever their background, to Christ?

Reaching Out

Our Father, please help me to be an irresistible heavenly fragrance that You can use to call to the many hungry hearts You bring into my life every day and draw them to Christ. Amen.

Afterword

In Chapter 22 of Numbers, there is a remarkable story that makes a hero out of a talking donkey—not exactly your typical Bible story! If anything, you'd expect something like that to be in the story of Noah, perhaps one of the elephants saying, "Hurry up, I just know the rain is going to start soon!" Instead, we have Numbers 22: 28-35 chronicling the account of how God gave a donkey the ability to speak to help accomplish His will—I invite you to read the chapter to see it for yourself.

But what's the point? How does it relate to reclaiming the table, bringing the family closer together, and strengthening our love for God? The point is this, if God can use a tired old donkey to save a wayward prophet and get him back on track, how much more can He use something as beautiful and meaningful as sharing a meal to accomplish His will for your family.

This devotional is a way to draw families closer to God and to one another. It is written to strengthen the meaning and understanding of the family table, unleash the subtle, yet considerable power of mealtime, and create a homegrown setting where the heart of heaven can beat freely with the love of God—around the family table. To maximize its effectiveness, it is important for each family member to shut the world out and be "all in" so they can focus, appreciate one another and their unique contributions to the meal, and the devotional experience. That means the television, mobile phones, iPads, and other electronic distractions (pick a device) must be set aside during mealtime. It is important to gather at the table around a healthy dinner, but with the realization that no matter how mouthwatering, the family table is more than a meal because it nourishes our relationships with God and one another.

As you share the meditations of this devotional and ponder their message, it is important for everyone's insight and perspective to be respected, appreciated, and embraced. No one person has all the understanding or all the answers except our Lord, and so He gave us each other to help us grow in His grace and love. Be open to the other perspectives, experiences, and ideas that are shared as you discuss the meaning of the meditation and how it applies to each of you. The exchange of ideas encourages all of us to be more and appreciate both the vision of others as well as our differences and commonalities.

Be open to learning, to "Reaching in" and digging deeper, and encourage each family member to offer their insight into the ideas offered and their interpretation of the Scripture that is shared. This way, sharing in the devotional will not only foster intentional and heartfelt relationships among family members, but also begin to form a godly tradition—a spiritual discipline that can grow across generations and bear fruit for years strengthening and knitting hearts together.

Again, this devotional is crafted with depth in mind as opposed to breadth. Its meditations are brief but thought provoking and designed to be savored with both the mind and the heart. The "Reaching In" ideas compliment the meditations and similarly, should be approached with an eye to the way the day's devotion applies to your life. The prayer, written to help reach out to the Lord, speaks for itself but do not hesitate to let it speak for you...

All of these thoughts, ideas, and inspirations come together to light your heart with the love of God and rekindle the meaning and ministry of the family table. So, as you share this spiritual meal and nourish your heart and soul, remember, just as it is the relationship between all the ingredients that make a family meal mouthwatering, it is the relationship between all of you that makes a family. But never forget the most important single ingredient—the recipe for life rises or falls because of our relationship with God through Jesus Christ. And, if you will, it is seasoned with God's grace and our faith as lived in our daily actions, especially with respect to our relationship to one another.

Having said that, which room in the house do you feel facilitates the most meaningful relationships—that is to say, which room do you consider the most crucial? Some might argue for the living room or family room, as it's where most people congregate and is seen as the common hub of the house. However, I firmly believe it's the kitchen. Why? Because it's in the kitchen that relationships deepen, and family members are nourished both physically and spiritually.

Sadly, however, the cherished family mealtime has become all but absent in today's world, and that treasured setting where parents and children once bonded over quality moments has found its way onto the endangered species list (so-to-speak). And as quality time at the family table has become more and more distant, so have meaningful relationships between parents and children. Parents need to observe what is happening in their children's lives fully, and children need to learn the surpassing value of their parents' guidance and wisdom. I strongly believe that a significant portion of the violence and social turmoil we witness today, along with the breakdown of the family unit and society itself, can be attributed to the dwindling time spent together in the heart of the home: the kitchen.

The physical aspect is evident; we all require sustenance to survive. But the spiritual nourishment served in the kitchen is even more vital. It's where family members truly connect, where parents can impart wisdom and mentor their children, and where children learn about life from their parents and siblings. It's a place where parents can observe and glean what's happening in their children's lives and speak into issues and questions as they see fit.

The kitchen also serves as a space where friends gather for a few hours and leave as family.

My motivation in writing this book is to offer families a chance to reclaim some of that precious time in the kitchen, fostering reflection on what truly matters in life. It's important to remember that "the family that prays together stays together," and by extension, sharing good food can provide an enticing incentive for families to rediscover the warmth of the most vital room in the house: the kitchen.

I hope that this journey has been fruitful for you and that the act of coming together for dinner as a family extends beyond this devotional, weaving itself into the very fabric of your life. It's time to "reclaim the table."

Recipes from Readers

These are recipes from friends and people I cherish. There is nothing like food to draw us together across the kitchen table. Use these—and enjoy!

Rigatoni Alla Bolognese

- 1lb of ground beef (select meat with higher fat content for more flavor)
- 28-oz can of San Marzano tomato puree or crushed tomatoes
- 3 tbsp. of olive oil
- 4 cloves of garlic, chopped
- 1 small yellow onion, diced
- 1 carrot, finely chopped
- 1 celery stalk, finely chopped

- Pinch of red pepper flakes
- Salt and ground black pepper, to taste
- 3 basil leaves, torn into pieces
- 1lb of Rigatoni Pasta

1. Heat the olive oil in a large, deep pan and sauté the onion, celery, and carrot until tender. Then add garlic and red pepper flakes. Stir to release the flavor.
2. Add the chopped meat and break it up with the back of a fork as it cooks.
3. Once the meat has browned, stir in the tomatoes. Season with salt and pepper. Add a small amount of water to the tomato can to grab any remaining tomato sauce. Add it to the pot.
4. Increase heat and bring to a lively simmer, stirring so the meat doesn't stick to the pot. Reduce heat and cover. Simmer for 45 minutes or more, stirring often. If the sauce thickens too much, adjust the consistency by adding a little water.
5. In a pot of boiling salted water, cook 1 pound of Rigatoni for 7 minutes or until "al dente".
6. Before removing the sauce from the stove, stir in the basil.

7. Pour out the boiled water, keeping the pasta in the pot, and proceed to introduce the sauce into the same pot alongside the pasta. Give it a good stir.
8. Serve with grated cheese and crushed red pepper flakes.

Genets (Anisette Cookies)

For the Cookies:
- 5 cups of all-purpose flour (more if dough is too wet or sticky)
- 1 cup of granulated sugar
- 5 tsp of baking powder
- Pinch of Salt
- 1 cup of vegetable oil
- 1 cup of milk
- 2 tsp of fresh lemon juice
- 2 eggs

For the Icing:
- 2 cups of confectioners' sugar
- Anisette liqueur or extract (add as much as it needs to be thinned)
- Nonpareil sprinkles

Make the cookies: Preheat oven to 350°

1. Combine all ingredients in large bowl
2. Dough may be a bit wet. If so, add a small amount of flour
3. Take 1 tablespoon of dough and form ball for each cookie
4. Place on cookie sheet coated with cooking spray
5. Bake until set but not brown for about 10-12 minutes.

Make the icing:

6. Mixing bowl
7. paper Wax

Mix all ingredients well with a hand mixer.
Dip cooled cookies one by one, sprinkle and place on drying rack or wax paper

Pasta Alla Mario

- 1 Cup of Grape tomatoes
- 3 Garlic cloves, chopped
- Extra Virgin olive Oil
- 1 Pound of Spaghetti
- 1/2 Cup of Italian Season Croutons (preferable)
- 1/4 Cup of Pecorino Romano grated cheese
- 1 Teaspoon Salt
- 5 Fresh Basil Leaves
- Shrimp or chicken optional

1. In a pot of boiling salted water, precook 1 pound of spaghetti for 6 minutes or until "al dente."
2. In a pan, sauté chopped garlic in olive oil for 1 minute,
3. Cut grape or cherry tomatoes lengthwise, add to the simmering garlic and oil, and cook until tomatoes are soft; add salt, then press down on tomatoes to expel the juices.
4. Add 1/2 cup of croutons to the pan and mix together.
5. Optional step: add cooked, cleaned shrimp to pan and heat for 3 minutes, occasionally mixing
6. Drain pasta and add to a heated pan with simmering ingredients; mix together, and add pecorino Romano grated cheese to the pan; garnish with fresh basil leaves; you are ready to serve.
7. Pour a glass of Pinot Grigio Santa Margherita and enjoy...

Orzo Pasta Salad

- 1lb orzo pasta
- 4-5 mini cucumbers
- 4-5 roma tomatoes
- 1 can black olives
- 1/4 of a red onion
- 1 package feta cheese

For the dressing:
- Juice of 2 lemons

- 1/4 cup olive oil
- 1/4 tsp onion powder
- 1/4 tsp garlic powder
- Salt to taste

1. Cook the orzo in salted water, drain, and rinse with cold water.
2. Cut cucumbers and tomatoes into small cubes.
3. Cut red onion and olives into thin slices.
4. Once the orzo is cooled completely, add it and the veggies to a large bowl.
5. In a separate container, whisk together the juice of 2 lemons, the garlic powder, onion power, and salt to taste.
6. Add the dressing to the bowl of pasta and veggies and toss together.
7. Top with crumbled feta cheese.
8. Enjoy!

Notes

Notes

Notes

Notes

Notes

www.ingramcontent.com/pod-product-compliance
Lightning Source LLC
LaVergne TN
LVHW070938070526
838199LV00035B/649